Introduction

The world of transportation is undergoing a transformative shift, heralded by the advent of autonomous travel technologies. At the forefront of this evolution is Autonomous World Level 3, a pivotal stage in the development of self-driving vehicles. To understand its significance, we must first define what Autonomous World Level 3 entails. This level of autonomy, as defined by the Society of Automotive Engineers (SAE), allows the vehicle to handle all aspects of driving in certain conditions without human intervention, but with the expectation that the human driver will respond to requests to intervene. In essence, it represents a hybrid stage where the vehicle can perform most driving tasks independently, yet still requires a human fallback in complex scenarios.

The importance and impact of autonomous travel on modern society cannot be overstated. Autonomous vehicles promise to revolutionize the way we perceive and interact with transportation. They offer the potential to significantly reduce traffic accidents, the vast majority of which are caused by human error. By relying on sophisticated sensors, artificial intelligence, and real-time data processing, these vehicles can make split-second decisions with a level of precision and consistency that humans cannot match. Additionally, autonomous travel can enhance mobility for individuals who are unable to drive, such as the elderly and disabled, thereby fostering greater independence and inclusion.

Moreover, the environmental impact of autonomous vehicles is another critical consideration. These vehicles can be optimized for fuel efficiency and reduced emissions, contributing to a more sustainable future. The shift towards autonomous travel also has the potential to reshape urban landscapes, reduce congestion, and improve the overall quality of life in cities around the world. Just as smartphones revolutionized communication and access to information, autonomous vehicles are poised to redefine our relationship with transportation.

To fully appreciate the advancements of Autonomous World Level 3, it is essential to trace the evolution of autonomous technology from its early stages. The journey began with Level 1 autonomy, which introduced basic driver assistance features such as adaptive cruise control and lane-keeping assistance. These systems provided incremental improvements in safety and convenience but required constant human oversight. Level 2 autonomy marked a significant leap forward, with vehicles capable of managing multiple driving tasks simultaneously, such as steering and acceleration, though still under the vigilant eye of the driver.

As we progressed towards 2024, the leap to Level 3 autonomy represents a monumental stride in technology and innovation. This level encapsulates the culmination of years of research, development, and rigorous testing. The path from Level 1 to Level 3 has been characterized by numerous breakthroughs in sensor technology, machine learning algorithms, and the integration of advanced computing power. Each stage of this journey has brought us closer to a future where autonomous vehicles are not just a novelty but a ubiquitous reality on our roads.

The introduction of Autonomous World Level 3 is a testament to the relentless pursuit of innovation in the transportation sector. It is poised to bring about profound changes in safety, accessibility, environmental sustainability, and urban planning. Understanding its development and impact provides us with a glimpse into the future of travel, where the fusion of technology and mobility creates a seamless, efficient, and safer world.

Understanding Level 3 Autonomous Driving

Definition and Features of Level 3 Autonomy:

Level 3 autonomous driving, as defined by the Society of Automotive Engineers (SAE), represents a significant milestone in the evolution of self-driving technology. At this level, a vehicle can perform all driving tasks within certain conditions, such as highway driving, without human intervention. However, it requires the driver to be ready to take control when requested by the system. This conditional automation is characterized by the vehicle's ability to make decisions based on real-time data, such as navigating traffic, adjusting speed, and changing lanes autonomously. The defining feature of Level 3 autonomy is the transition from partial to conditional automation, where the system handles dynamic driving tasks but still involves the human driver as a fallback.

Differences between Level 3 and Previous Levels (Level 1 and Level 2):

The progression from Level 1 to Level 3 autonomy showcases a remarkable technological evolution. Level 1 autonomy includes basic driver assistance systems, such as adaptive cruise control and lane-keeping assist, which support the driver by managing single tasks but require constant human supervision. Level 2 autonomy advances further by integrating multiple assistance features, allowing the vehicle to control both steering and acceleration/deceleration simultaneously. However, the driver must remain fully engaged and ready to take over at any moment.

In contrast, Level 3 autonomy elevates the driving experience by enabling the vehicle to handle all driving operations under specific conditions, thus reducing the driver's workload significantly. This shift from partial automation to conditional automation represents a paradigm change, as it introduces the capability for the vehicle to make informed driving decisions autonomously, while still necessitating human intervention in complex or unanticipated situations.

Key Technologies Enabling Level 3 Autonomy:

The realization of Level 3 autonomous driving hinges on a confluence of advanced technologies. Critical among these are sensors, artificial intelligence (AI), and machine learning. Sensors, including LiDAR (Light Detection and Ranging), radar, and high-resolution cameras, provide the vehicle with a comprehensive understanding of its surroundings by continuously capturing detailed environmental data. These sensors detect and interpret various elements such as road conditions, obstacles, and other vehicles, enabling the autonomous system to navigate safely and efficiently.

AI and machine learning algorithms process the vast amounts of data generated by these sensors, facilitating real-time decision-making. Machine learning models are trained to recognize patterns and predict outcomes, which enhances the vehicle's ability to respond to dynamic driving scenarios. For instance, AI can assess traffic flow, predict the behavior of other road users, and optimize routes for efficiency and safety. The integration of these technologies creates a robust framework that underpins the functionality and reliability of Level 3 autonomous vehicles.

Major Vehicle OEMs and Their Innovations:

The development of Level 3 autonomous vehicles has seen significant contributions from major vehicle Original Equipment Manufacturers (OEMs), each bringing unique innovations to the table. Companies like Tesla, BMW, and Mercedes-Benz are at the forefront of this technological race, pushing the boundaries of what is possible in autonomous driving.

Tesla, known for its groundbreaking work in electric vehicles and autonomous technology, has been instrumental in advancing driver assistance systems. Its Autopilot and Full Self-Driving (FSD) features incorporate advanced AI and machine learning capabilities, positioning Tesla as a leader in the industry.

BMW has made significant strides with its iNEXT platform, which is designed to offer Level 3 autonomy. The company's focus on integrating cutting-edge sensor technology and high-performance computing ensures a seamless and safe driving experience.

Mercedes-Benz has introduced the Drive Pilot system, which exemplifies Level 3 autonomy by allowing drivers to delegate driving tasks to the vehicle under certain conditions. This system is a testament to Mercedes-Benz's commitment to innovation and safety in autonomous driving.

Case Studies of Leading Automakers (e.g., Tesla, BMW, Mercedes-Benz):

Examining specific case studies of leading automakers provides valuable insights into the practical applications and advancements in Level 3 autonomous driving. For example, Tesla's approach to autonomy is characterized by its use of over-the-air software updates, which continuously enhance the capabilities of its vehicles. Tesla's Autopilot system leverages a combination of cameras, radar, and ultrasonic sensors, coupled with AI algorithms, to deliver a highly sophisticated driving experience.

BMW's iNEXT vehicle exemplifies the company's dedication to autonomous innovation. By integrating LiDAR, radar, and camera systems with AI-powered decision-making processes, BMW ensures that its vehicles can navigate complex driving environments autonomously. The iNEXT platform's ability to handle highway driving autonomously while allowing for human intervention when necessary is a hallmark of Level 3 autonomy.

Mercedes-Benz's Drive Pilot system is another notable example. This system, available in the S-Class and EQS models, allows for hands-free driving in certain conditions, such as on highways. The Drive Pilot system utilizes a suite of sensors, including LiDAR and cameras, to monitor the vehicle's surroundings and ensure safe operation. Mercedes-Benz's emphasis on safety and reliability is evident in its rigorous testing and validation processes, which are crucial for the successful deployment of Level 3 autonomous technology.

Timeline of Development and Introduction of Level 3 Vehicles:

The journey towards Level 3 autonomous vehicles has been marked by incremental advancements and significant milestones. The early 2010s saw the introduction of Level 1 and Level 2 driver assistance systems, which laid the groundwork for more advanced autonomous capabilities. By the mid-2010s, major OEMs began investing heavily in research and development to push the boundaries of autonomous driving.

The late 2010s and early 2020s witnessed the emergence of pilot programs and limited deployments of Level 3 technology. Companies like Audi introduced the A8 with Traffic Jam Pilot, one of the first production vehicles to offer Level 3 capabilities. Meanwhile, regulatory bodies around the world began developing frameworks to support the safe deployment of autonomous vehicles.

As we approached 2024, the pace of development accelerated, with multiple automakers announcing plans to launch Level 3 autonomous vehicles. The timeline reflects a decade of continuous innovation, rigorous testing, and collaboration between industry stakeholders and regulatory authorities. Each step along this journey has brought us closer to a future where Level 3 autonomous vehicles are a common sight on our roads, revolutionizing the way we travel and interact with our environment.

The Technology Behind Autonomous Vehicles

The backbone of autonomous vehicles lies in their advanced sensor technology, which enables them to perceive and interact with their surroundings. This suite of sensors includes LiDAR, radar, cameras, and ultrasonic sensors, each playing a crucial role in the vehicle's ability to navigate safely and efficiently.

LiDAR (Light Detection and Ranging) uses laser pulses to create detailed, three-dimensional maps of the environment. By measuring the time it takes for the laser to return after hitting an object, LiDAR generates precise distance data, allowing the vehicle to identify obstacles, road edges, and other critical features.

Radar (Radio Detection and Ranging) complements LiDAR by providing robust detection capabilities in various weather conditions. Radar systems use radio waves to detect objects and their velocities, making them particularly useful for tracking moving vehicles and pedestrians.

Cameras are essential for capturing visual information. They can recognize traffic signals, road signs, lane markings, and other vehicles. High-resolution cameras, often combined with image recognition algorithms, allow the vehicle to interpret complex visual cues.

Ultrasonic sensors are typically used for close-range detection, such as parking assistance. These sensors emit sound waves and measure the time taken for the echo to return, helping the vehicle detect nearby objects at low speeds.

The integration of these diverse sensors through data fusion techniques is critical for creating a coherent and accurate representation of the environment. By combining data from multiple sources, the autonomous system can cross-verify information, reduce uncertainties, and enhance overall situational awareness. Real-time processing of this data is achieved through high-performance computing units, which ensure that the vehicle can respond swiftly and accurately to dynamic driving conditions.

Artificial Intelligence and Machine Learning:

Artificial Intelligence (AI) and Machine Learning (ML) are the intellectual engines driving the decision-making processes of autonomous vehicles. These technologies enable the vehicle to analyze sensor data, predict future scenarios, and make informed decisions on the road.

Algorithms and neural networks form the core of AI systems in autonomous vehicles. These complex mathematical models are designed to process vast amounts of data and recognize patterns, allowing the vehicle to understand and react to its environment. For instance, neural networks can identify pedestrians, cyclists, and other vehicles, as well as anticipate their movements to avoid collisions.

Data training and simulations are essential for developing reliable autonomous systems.

Autonomous vehicles are trained using extensive datasets that include a variety of driving scenarios, from urban traffic to rural roads. These datasets are used to teach the AI how to handle different situations, enhancing its ability to generalize and perform well in real-world conditions. Simulations further augment this process by allowing developers to test and refine algorithms in a virtual environment before deploying them on actual roads. This approach accelerates development and ensures safety by identifying and addressing potential issues early on.

Communication Systems:

Communication systems are another vital component of autonomous vehicle technology, enabling vehicles to interact with each other and with infrastructure. V2X (Vehicle-to-Everything) communication encompasses various types of connectivity, including Vehicle-to-Vehicle (V2V), Vehicle-to-Infrastructure (V2I), and Vehicle-to-Pedestrian (V2P). These systems allow vehicles to share information about their speed, location, and direction, enhancing their ability to anticipate and respond to potential hazards.

V2V communication enables vehicles to exchange data directly with one another, providing real-time updates on traffic conditions, road hazards, and accidents. This information helps vehicles make better decisions, such as adjusting speed to avoid congestion or rerouting to evade obstacles.

V2I communication involves the exchange of data between vehicles and roadside infrastructure, such as traffic lights and road signs. This connectivity allows vehicles to receive information about traffic signal timings, road closures, and other important updates, improving traffic flow and safety. V2P communication enhances safety by enabling vehicles to detect and communicate with pedestrians and cyclists, reducing the risk of accidents.

The role of 5G and future connectivity technologies is pivotal in advancing V2X communication. 5G networks offer low latency, high bandwidth, and reliable connectivity, essential for the rapid exchange of data required by autonomous vehicles. With 5G, vehicles can process and respond to information in near real-time, making autonomous driving safer and more efficient. Future connectivity technologies will further expand these capabilities, supporting the development of more sophisticated and reliable autonomous systems.

The technology behind autonomous vehicles is a complex and interconnected web of sensors, AI, and communication systems. These components work together seamlessly to enable vehicles to perceive their environment, make intelligent decisions, and interact with other road users and infrastructure. As these technologies continue to evolve, they will drive the advancement of autonomous vehicles, bringing us closer to a future of safer, more efficient, and fully autonomous transportation.

Autonomous Air Mobility

Electric Air Taxis:

Electric air taxis, often referred to as eVTOL (electric Vertical Takeoff and Landing) aircraft, represent a groundbreaking advancement in urban transportation. These aircraft are designed to take off and land vertically, much like a helicopter, but are powered by electric propulsion systems. This technology offers several advantages, including reduced noise levels, lower emissions, and the ability to operate in congested urban environments without the need for extensive runway infrastructure.

Key players in the air taxi market are pioneering this innovative mode of transportation. Joby Aviation is a leader in the field, developing eVTOL aircraft with the vision of providing fast, efficient, and environmentally friendly urban air mobility solutions. Their aircraft are designed to carry passengers over short to medium distances, significantly reducing travel times compared to traditional ground transportation. Volocopter is another prominent company, focusing on creating safe and reliable air taxi services with their multi-rotor eVTOL designs. Their aircraft are envisioned to provide on-demand air taxi services, seamlessly integrating with existing transportation networks to offer a new dimension of urban mobility.

A notable case study highlighting the potential of air taxi services is the upcoming Paris 2024 Olympics, where air taxis are set to make their debut. This event will serve as a significant milestone, showcasing the feasibility and benefits of eVTOL technology in a real-world, high-profile setting. The introduction of air taxis during the Olympics will provide a practical demonstration of how this technology can alleviate traffic congestion, enhance mobility, and offer a unique and efficient transportation option for attendees and athletes.

Infrastructure and Regulatory Challenges:

The widespread adoption of autonomous air mobility faces several infrastructure and regulatory challenges. Air traffic management for urban air mobility is a critical concern, as the introduction of eVTOL aircraft will require a new system for managing low-altitude air traffic in densely populated areas. This involves developing advanced air traffic control systems that can handle the increased volume and complexity of urban air traffic, ensuring the safe and efficient movement of air taxis alongside traditional aircraft.

Regulatory frameworks and safety standards are also essential for the successful implementation of autonomous air mobility. Governments and aviation authorities must establish comprehensive regulations to govern the operation of eVTOL aircraft, addressing issues such as airspace integration, pilot training, vehicle certification, and operational safety. These regulations must balance the need for innovation with stringent safety requirements to protect passengers and the public.

Integration with Existing Transportation Networks:

The integration of air taxis with existing transportation networks is crucial for creating a cohesive urban mobility ecosystem. Intermodal transportation involves the seamless connection of different modes of transport, such as ground vehicles, public transit, and air taxis, to provide a holistic travel experience. Air taxis can play a significant role in urban mobility by offering rapid and flexible transportation options that complement traditional ground-based systems.

Future visions of seamless travel across land and air envision a scenario where passengers can effortlessly switch between various modes of transport. For example, a commuter could travel from their home to a nearby vertiport (a landing and takeoff site for eVTOL aircraft), take an air taxi to a city center, and then use a shared autonomous vehicle for the last mile of their journey. This integrated approach aims to minimize travel times, reduce congestion, and enhance the overall efficiency of urban transportation networks.

Autonomous air mobility, particularly through the development of electric air taxis, holds the promise of revolutionizing urban transportation. The advancements in eVTOL technology by companies like Joby Aviation and Volocopter, coupled with real-world implementations like the Paris 2024 Olympics, demonstrate the potential of this innovative mode of travel. However, addressing infrastructure and regulatory challenges and ensuring seamless integration with existing transportation networks are critical steps toward realizing the full potential of autonomous air mobility. As these hurdles are overcome, we can anticipate a future where urban travel is faster, more efficient, and more environmentally friendly, transcending the limitations of current transportation systems.

Economic Impact of Autonomous Travel

The autonomous travel market presents vast economic opportunities and is poised for significant growth in the coming years. Global market size and growth forecasts indicate that the autonomous vehicle sector, encompassing both automotive and aviation industries, is expected to expand rapidly. According to industry analysts, the global autonomous vehicle market is projected to reach over $556 billion by 2026, driven by advancements in technology, increased consumer acceptance, and supportive regulatory frameworks. The demand for autonomous vehicles is not limited to passenger cars; it extends to logistics, public transportation, and even personal air travel, creating a diverse and expansive market landscape.

Various economic sectors are affected by autonomous travel, including automotive, aviation, and logistics. In the automotive industry, manufacturers are investing heavily in developing self-driving technologies, leading to the creation of new business models and revenue streams. Autonomous travel also promises to revolutionize the aviation sector, particularly with the advent of eVTOL aircraft for urban air mobility. In logistics, autonomous delivery vehicles and drones are set to transform supply chain operations, offering faster, more efficient, and cost-effective solutions. This cross-sector impact highlights the transformative potential of autonomous travel on the global economy.

Investment and Funding Trends:

The autonomous technology sector has attracted substantial investment and funding from key players in the industry. Key investors and venture capital trends reveal a strong interest in companies developing autonomous systems. Major tech giants, traditional automotive manufacturers, and specialized startups are receiving significant financial backing. Notable investors include firms like SoftBank, which has invested billions into autonomous vehicle startups, and Alphabet's venture capital arm, GV, which has funded several innovative companies in this space.

Case studies of successful funding rounds and IPOs illustrate the vibrant investment landscape. For instance, Waymo, the autonomous driving subsidiary of Alphabet, raised $2.25 billion in its first external funding round in 2020, underscoring investor confidence in its technology and business model. Another example is the IPO of Luminar Technologies, a leading provider of LiDAR sensors, which went public in 2020 with a valuation of over $3 billion. These cases highlight the substantial capital flowing into the autonomous sector, driving innovation and market expansion.

Job Creation and Disruption:

The rise of autonomous travel will lead to both job creation and disruption across various industries. New job roles in autonomous vehicle technology and maintenance are emerging, requiring specialized skills and expertise. These roles include positions such as AI and machine learning engineers, sensor technology specialists, autonomous system testers, and maintenance technicians for autonomous fleets. The need for a skilled workforce to develop, manage, and maintain autonomous systems will create numerous high-tech job opportunities.

However, the impact on traditional driving jobs cannot be overlooked. As autonomous vehicles become more prevalent, roles such as truck drivers, taxi operators, and delivery personnel may face significant disruption. To mitigate these impacts, potential strategies include reskilling and upskilling programs to help affected workers transition into new roles within the autonomous technology sector. For example, training programs can focus on equipping traditional drivers with skills in autonomous vehicle operation and maintenance, ensuring they can continue to find employment in a transforming industry.

The economic impact of autonomous travel is multifaceted, encompassing market growth, investment trends, and workforce changes. The global market for autonomous vehicles is set to expand significantly, driven by technological advancements and broad sectoral applications. Investment in autonomous technology continues to grow, fueling innovation and development. While the advent of autonomous travel will create new job opportunities, it will also disrupt traditional driving roles, necessitating proactive measures to support affected workers. As we navigate this transformative period, the economic landscape will continue to evolve, reflecting the profound influence of autonomous travel on society.

Safety, Security, and Ethical Considerations

The safety of autonomous vehicles is paramount, and rigorous safety standards and testing protocols have been established to ensure their reliability and performance. Crash test standards for autonomous vehicles are designed to evaluate how these vehicles respond in various accident scenarios. These standards often include simulations of frontal, side, and rear-end collisions to assess the impact on vehicle integrity and passenger safety. Additionally, real-world testing scenarios are crucial for understanding how autonomous vehicles perform in diverse driving conditions, such as heavy traffic, adverse weather, and complex urban environments.

Incident analysis and continuous improvement strategies are integral to maintaining and enhancing the safety of autonomous vehicles. When an incident occurs, detailed investigations are conducted to determine the cause and identify potential system failures. This analysis informs the development of updated safety protocols and system enhancements. Continuous improvement strategies involve regularly updating the vehicle's software, refining algorithms, and incorporating lessons learned from previous incidents to prevent future occurrences. These proactive measures ensure that autonomous vehicles become progressively safer over time.

Cybersecurity in Autonomous Vehicles:

As autonomous vehicles become more connected and reliant on software, cybersecurity emerges as a critical concern. Protecting autonomous systems from hacking and cyber threats is essential to ensure the safety and reliability of these vehicles. Autonomous vehicles use a range of sensors, communication systems, and onboard computers, all of which are potential targets for cyber-attacks. To safeguard these systems, robust cybersecurity measures must be implemented, including encryption, secure coding practices, and regular vulnerability assessments.

Case studies of cybersecurity breaches and responses highlight the importance of effective cybersecurity strategies. For example, in 2015, researchers demonstrated a remote hack of a Jeep Cherokee, gaining control of its steering, brakes, and transmission. This incident prompted Fiat Chrysler to issue a recall and implement software updates to enhance the vehicle's security. Another example involves Tesla, which has faced several hacking attempts. Tesla's proactive approach includes regular security updates, a bug bounty program, and partnerships with cybersecurity experts to continually improve the resilience of its vehicles. These case studies underscore the necessity of ongoing vigilance and adaptation in the face of evolving cyber threats.

Ethical and Legal Implications:

The deployment of autonomous vehicles raises significant ethical and legal implications that must be carefully considered. Ethical dilemmas in autonomous decision-making arise when vehicles must make complex choices in critical situations. For instance, in the event of an unavoidable accident, an autonomous vehicle may need to decide between minimizing harm to its passengers or to pedestrians. These scenarios, often referred to as "trolley problems," present moral challenges that require a clear ethical framework for programming autonomous decision-making systems. The development of such frameworks involves collaboration between ethicists, engineers, policymakers, and the public to ensure that the decisions made by autonomous vehicles align with societal values.

Legal liability in accidents involving autonomous vehicles is another complex issue. Determining fault in incidents where autonomous vehicles are involved can be challenging, as responsibility may lie with the vehicle manufacturer, software developer, or the vehicle owner. Legal frameworks need to address questions of liability and accountability, ensuring that victims receive fair compensation while fostering innovation and adoption of autonomous technology.

Recent legislative efforts in various countries are beginning to establish guidelines for liability, but this remains an evolving area of law that will need continual refinement as autonomous technology advances.

The integration of autonomous vehicles into society brings with it critical safety, security, and ethical considerations. Ensuring robust safety standards and testing protocols is essential for the safe operation of these vehicles. Addressing cybersecurity threats requires a proactive and adaptive approach to protect autonomous systems from malicious attacks. Furthermore, navigating the ethical and legal implications of autonomous decision-making and liability is vital for gaining public trust and establishing a clear regulatory framework. As the autonomous vehicle landscape continues to evolve, these considerations will play a pivotal role in shaping the future of transportation.

Public Perception and Adoption

Understanding consumer attitudes towards autonomous vehicles is crucial for their widespread adoption. Surveys and studies consistently show a mix of excitement and skepticism among the public. Many consumers appreciate the potential benefits of autonomous vehicles, such as increased safety, reduced traffic congestion, and greater convenience. However, trust remains a significant barrier. According to a 2023 survey by the American Automobile Association (AAA), while 52% of respondents expressed interest in self-driving technology, only 22% stated they would feel safe riding in an autonomous vehicle.

Barriers to adoption include concerns over safety, cybersecurity, and the reliability of autonomous systems. Additionally, many consumers are hesitant due to a lack of understanding of how autonomous vehicles operate and how they interact with human drivers. Strategies to overcome these barriers involve rigorous safety testing, transparent communication about the capabilities and limitations of autonomous technology, and public demonstrations to showcase their reliability and safety in real-world scenarios.

Government and Policy Initiatives:

Government support and incentives for autonomous technology are pivotal in fostering adoption. Various governments worldwide are introducing policies to encourage the development and deployment of autonomous vehicles. In the United States, the Federal Automated Vehicles Policy outlines guidelines for the testing and deployment of autonomous vehicles, promoting innovation while ensuring safety. Financial incentives, such as grants and tax credits, are also being provided to companies developing autonomous technologies.

International collaboration and standardization efforts are essential to ensure interoperability and safety across borders. Organizations like the International Organization for Standardization (ISO) and the United Nations Economic Commission for Europe (UNECE) are working on creating global standards for autonomous vehicles. These efforts include harmonizing safety protocols, data sharing guidelines, and cybersecurity measures, which are crucial for the seamless integration of autonomous vehicles into the global transportation ecosystem.

Educational and Awareness Campaigns:

The role of education in promoting understanding and acceptance of autonomous vehicles cannot be overstated. Public education campaigns are essential to inform consumers about the benefits, safety features, and operational principles of autonomous vehicles. These campaigns help demystify the technology, addressing common misconceptions and building trust among potential users.

Case studies of successful awareness campaigns provide valuable insights. One notable example is the "Self-Driving Coalition for Safer Streets," a collaboration between major companies like Waymo, Ford, and Uber. This coalition aims to educate the public and policymakers about the safety and societal benefits of autonomous vehicles through workshops, public demonstrations, and informational websites. Another successful campaign is the UK's "MERGE Greenwich" project, which conducted extensive community engagement activities to gather feedback and educate residents about the potential impacts of autonomous vehicle trials in their area. These campaigns demonstrate the effectiveness of targeted education and community involvement in building public trust and acceptance.

The public perception and adoption of autonomous vehicles are influenced by a combination of consumer attitudes, government policies, and educational efforts. Addressing consumer concerns through transparent communication and demonstrating the safety and benefits of autonomous technology are essential steps towards widespread acceptance. Government initiatives, including support and incentives, along with international standardization efforts, provide a robust framework for the integration of autonomous vehicles. Finally, educational and awareness campaigns play a critical role in promoting understanding and trust, paving the way for a future where autonomous vehicles are a trusted and integral part of our transportation system.

Future of Autonomous Travel

The future of autonomous travel is bright, driven by continuous advancements in technology. One of the key areas of development is advances in AI and machine learning for higher levels of autonomy (Level 4 and Level 5). At Level 4, vehicles will be capable of operating without human intervention in most conditions, although a driver may still have the option to take control. At Level 5, the ultimate goal, vehicles will be fully autonomous, capable of navigating any environment without any human input. These advancements will rely heavily on more sophisticated AI algorithms and neural networks that can handle complex decision-making processes in real-time. Machine learning models will need to be trained on vast amounts of diverse driving data, enabling them to anticipate and react to a wide range of scenarios.

Another promising area is potential breakthroughs in battery technology and energy management. The efficiency and longevity of batteries are crucial for the widespread adoption of electric autonomous vehicles. Innovations such as solid-state batteries, which offer higher energy density and faster charging times, are expected to revolutionize the industry. Improved energy management systems will also play a vital role, optimizing power consumption and extending the range of autonomous vehicles. These advancements will not only make autonomous travel more practical but also more environmentally friendly.

Long-term Projections and Scenarios:

Looking ahead, the vision for 2030 and beyond in autonomous travel is filled with exciting possibilities. By 2030, it is expected that Level 4 autonomous vehicles will be commonplace in urban environments, significantly reducing traffic congestion and accidents caused by human error. Public transportation systems will also see a transformation, with autonomous buses and shuttles providing efficient and reliable service. Rural areas, too, will benefit from autonomous travel, improving accessibility and reducing isolation.

Speculative scenarios paint an even more futuristic picture, where autonomous technology extends beyond Earth. Concepts such as autonomous spaceships and interplanetary travel are no longer confined to the realm of science fiction. Companies like SpaceX and Blue Origin are already laying the groundwork for autonomous space travel, envisioning a future where robotic spacecraft can explore distant planets and moons independently. These autonomous explorers could pave the way for human colonization of other planets, with intelligent systems managing everything from navigation to life support.

Preparing for an Autonomous Future:

As we move towards a future dominated by autonomous travel, it is essential for individuals and businesses to prepare for widespread adoption. For individuals, staying informed about technological advancements and understanding how to interact with autonomous systems will be crucial. This includes learning about the safety features and operational principles of autonomous vehicles and adapting to new modes of transportation.

For businesses, the autonomous era presents numerous opportunities for innovation and entrepreneurship. Companies can develop new products and services tailored to the autonomous market, such as advanced sensors, AI software, and cybersecurity solutions. The logistics and delivery sectors, in particular, stand to benefit from autonomous technology, with the potential for significant cost savings and efficiency improvements. Additionally, businesses can explore the development of autonomous infrastructure, such as charging stations, maintenance facilities, and communication networks.

The future of autonomous travel is poised to bring transformative changes to our world. Emerging technologies and innovations in AI, machine learning, and battery technology will drive the development of higher levels of autonomy. Long-term projections envision a world where autonomous vehicles are ubiquitous, enhancing safety and efficiency in transportation. Speculative scenarios extend this vision to outer space, hinting at a future where autonomous technology enables interplanetary exploration. To prepare for this autonomous future, individuals and businesses must stay informed and embrace the opportunities for innovation and entrepreneurship. As we navigate this exciting era, the promise of autonomous travel will reshape our lives in ways we can only begin to imagine.

Conclusion

As we conclude our exploration of the world of autonomous travel, it's essential to recap the key points discussed throughout this book. We began by defining and understanding Autonomous World Level 3, a pivotal stage where vehicles can handle most driving tasks independently under certain conditions, while still requiring human intervention in complex scenarios. This level of autonomy marks a significant leap from the previous levels, bringing us closer to a future where autonomous vehicles are a common sight on our roads.

We delved into the technology behind autonomous vehicles, highlighting the critical role of advanced sensors, artificial intelligence, and machine learning. These technologies enable vehicles to perceive their surroundings, make informed decisions, and navigate safely and efficiently. We also examined the importance of robust cybersecurity measures to protect these sophisticated systems from potential threats.

The discussion extended to economic impacts, showcasing the market opportunities, investment trends, and the potential for job creation and disruption. We explored how autonomous travel could reshape various sectors, from automotive and aviation to logistics, while emphasizing the need for proactive strategies to address workforce changes.

Safety, security, and ethical considerations were another focal point, stressing the importance of rigorous safety standards, continuous improvement strategies, and ethical frameworks for autonomous decision-making. We also addressed the legal implications of autonomous vehicle incidents, highlighting the need for clear regulatory guidelines.

Public perception and adoption are crucial for the success of autonomous vehicles. We discussed consumer attitudes, government policies, and the role of educational campaigns in building trust and understanding. By fostering public awareness and addressing concerns, we can pave the way for broader acceptance of autonomous travel.

Looking ahead, the future of autonomous travel is filled with promise. Emerging technologies and innovations, such as advances in AI and battery technology, will drive the development of higher levels of autonomy. Long-term projections envision a world where autonomous vehicles are integral to urban mobility and even speculate on the potential for autonomous space travel.

Final thoughts on the transformative potential of Autonomous World Level 3 highlight its capacity to revolutionize transportation, enhance safety, and improve efficiency. By reducing human error, optimizing traffic flow, and providing new mobility solutions, autonomous vehicles can significantly impact our daily lives and urban landscapes.

In closing, a call to action for embracing the future of autonomous travel is vital. As individuals, staying informed and adapting to new technologies will prepare us for the changes ahead. For businesses, the autonomous era presents opportunities for innovation and growth. Policymakers and regulators must continue to develop supportive frameworks that encourage safe and sustainable adoption of autonomous vehicles.

The journey towards a fully autonomous world is not without its challenges, but the potential benefits are immense. By embracing this future, we can create a safer, more efficient, and more connected world, where autonomous travel is not just a technological advancement but a cornerstone of modern society.

Glossary of Key Terms and Concepts

- **Autonomous Vehicle (AV):** A vehicle capable of sensing its environment and operating without human intervention.

- **Level 1 Autonomy:** Basic driver assistance features such as adaptive cruise control and lane-keeping assist.

- **Level 2 Autonomy:** Advanced driver assistance systems that can control both steering and acceleration/deceleration simultaneously but require human oversight.

- **Level 3 Autonomy:** Conditional automation where the vehicle can handle most driving tasks independently under certain conditions, with the expectation that the human driver will respond to requests to intervene.

- **Level 4 Autonomy:** High automation where the vehicle can perform all driving tasks independently in most conditions, but human intervention may still be an option.

- Level 5 Autonomy: Full automation where the vehicle can operate independently in all conditions without any human intervention.

- eVTOL (Electric Vertical Takeoff and Landing): Aircraft that can take off and land vertically using electric propulsion, designed for urban air mobility.

- LiDAR (Light Detection and Ranging): A sensor technology that uses laser pulses to create detailed, three-dimensional maps of the environment.

- Radar (Radio Detection and Ranging): A sensor technology that uses radio waves to detect objects and their velocities.

- V2X (Vehicle-to-Everything) Communication: Technology that allows vehicles to communicate with each other and with infrastructure, including Vehicle-to-Vehicle (V2V), Vehicle-to-Infrastructure (V2I), and Vehicle-to-Pedestrian (V2P).

- Machine Learning: A subset of artificial intelligence that involves training algorithms to recognize patterns and make decisions based on data.

- **Neural Networks:** Computational models inspired by the human brain, used in machine learning to recognize patterns and process data.

 List of Major Companies and Stakeholders in the Autonomous Industry:

- **Waymo:** A subsidiary of Alphabet Inc. and a leader in autonomous driving technology.

- **Tesla:** An electric vehicle manufacturer known for its advanced driver-assistance systems and self-driving capabilities.

- **Uber Advanced Technologies Group (ATG):** A division of Uber focused on developing autonomous ride-sharing vehicles.

- **Cruise:** A subsidiary of General Motors, developing self-driving cars for urban environments.

- **Aurora:** A technology company specializing in self-driving software and hardware solutions.

- **Nuro:** A robotics company focused on autonomous delivery vehicles.

- **Zoox:** An autonomous vehicle company developing purpose-built, fully autonomous vehicles for ride-hailing.

- **Joby Aviation:** A leading company in the development of eVTOL aircraft for urban air mobility.

- **Volocopter:** A company specializing in eVTOL technology and urban air mobility solutions.

- **Mobileye:** An Intel subsidiary that provides advanced driver-assistance systems and autonomous driving technologies.

- **Aptiv:** A technology company that develops advanced safety, electrification, and autonomous driving solutions.

Further Reading and Resources for In-Depth Exploration

- "The Fourth Industrial Revolution" by Klaus Schwab: An insightful book on the impact of emerging technologies, including autonomous vehicles, on society and industry.

- "Autonomous Driving: How the Driverless Revolution Will Change the World" by Andreas Herrmann, Walter Brenner, and Rupert Stadler: A comprehensive exploration of the implications of autonomous vehicles on various aspects of life.

- SAE International: The Society of Automotive Engineers offers extensive resources and publications on automotive and autonomous vehicle standards (www.sae.org).

- IEEE Spectrum: A magazine and website providing news and analysis on the latest advancements in technology, including autonomous vehicles (spectrum.ieee.org).

- Waymo Blog: Official blog of Waymo, offering updates and insights into their autonomous vehicle projects (blog.waymo.com).

- Tesla Autopilot: Information and updates on Tesla's Autopilot and Full Self-Driving capabilities (www.tesla.com/autopilot).

- National Highway Traffic Safety Administration (NHTSA): U.S. government agency providing guidelines and information on vehicle safety and autonomous vehicle regulations (www.nhtsa.gov).

- International Transport Forum (ITF): An organization that explores transport policies and innovations, including autonomous vehicles (www.itf-oecd.org).

These appendices provide essential definitions, a list of key industry players, and resources for further exploration, enhancing the reader's understanding of the autonomous travel landscape and its future trajectory.

References

1. American Automobile Association (AAA) Survey, 2023. "Consumer Trust in Autonomous Vehicles." Available at: www.aaa.com/autonomous-survey

2. SAE International. "Taxonomy and Definitions for Terms Related to On-Road Motor Vehicle Automated Driving Systems." J3016_201806. Available at: www.sae.org/standards/content/j3016_201806

3. Federal Automated Vehicles Policy. U.S. Department of Transportation, 2020. Available at: www.transportation.gov/av/policy

4. "The Fourth Industrial Revolution" by Klaus Schwab. Crown Publishing Group, 2017.

5. "Autonomous Driving: How the Driverless Revolution Will Change the World" by Andreas Herrmann, Walter Brenner, and Rupert Stadler. Emerald Publishing, 2018.

6. IEEE Spectrum. "Advances in AI and Machine Learning for Autonomous Vehicles." Available at: spectrum.ieee.org/autonomous-vehicles

7. Waymo Blog. "Waymo's Journey to Level 5 Autonomy." Available at: blog.waymo.com

8. Tesla Autopilot. "Understanding Tesla's Full Self-Driving Capabilities." Available at: www.tesla.com/autopilot

9. National Highway Traffic Safety Administration (NHTSA). "Autonomous Vehicle Guidelines and Safety Standards." Available at: www.nhtsa.gov/technology-innovation/automated-vehicles-safety

10. International Transport Forum (ITF). "Transport Innovation for Sustainable Development: The Case of Autonomous Vehicles." Available at: www.itf-oecd.org

11. SoftBank Vision Fund. "Investment Trends in Autonomous Technology." Available at: www.softbank.jp/en/corp/vision-fund

12. Alphabet Inc. (GV). "Funding Innovations in Autonomous Systems." Available at: www.gv.com

13. "Self-Driving Coalition for Safer Streets." Awareness Campaign Materials, 2021. Available at: www.selfdrivingcoalition.org

14. "MERGE Greenwich Project". Community Engagement and Public Perception Report, 2020. Available at: www.mergegreenwich.com

15. Fiat Chrysler Automobiles (FCA). "Response to Cybersecurity Vulnerabilities in Connected Vehicles." Recall Report, 2015. Available at: www.fca.com/cybersecurity-recall

16. Tesla's Bug Bounty Program. Details and Case Studies on Cybersecurity Enhancements. Available at: www.tesla.com/bug-bounty

17. Joby Aviation. "Advancements in eVTOL Technology for Urban Air Mobility." Technical Papers, 2023. Available at: www.jobyaviation.com/research

18. Volocopter. "eVTOL Innovations and Market Impact." White Papers, 2023. Available at: www.volocopter.com/whitepapers

19. SpaceX. "Autonomous Space Travel: Current Projects and Future Visions."

Technical Report, 2022. Available at:
www.spacex.com/autonomous-space

20. Blue Origin. "Exploring Autonomous
Spacecraft for Interplanetary Missions."
Research Papers, 2022. Available at:
www.blueorigin.com/research

21. International Organization for
Standardization (ISO). "Standards for
Autonomous Vehicle Safety and
Interoperability." Available at: www.iso.org

22. United Nations Economic Commission for
Europe (UNECE). "Global Standards for
Autonomous Vehicles." Available at:
www.unece.org

23. U.S. Department of Labor. "The Future of
Work in an Autonomous Vehicle Era."
Research Report, 2023. Available at:
www.dol.gov/autonomous-future

24. Bloomberg NEF. "Market Projections for Autonomous Vehicles." Industry Analysis, 2023. Available at: www.bnef.com/autonomous-vehicles

www.ingramcontent.com/pod-product-compliance
Lightning Source LLC
Chambersburg PA
CBHW070900070326
40690CB00009B/1924